E

1955

News for every
day of the year

Compiled by Hugh Morrison

Ford Edsel

Montpelier Publishing
London

Cover images: Front cover(clockwise): President Dwight D. Eisenhower. Project Mercury astronauts. The Austin-Morris Mini. The Dalai Lama. Rear cover: (clockwise): Elizabeth Taylor. The Ford Falcon. Chairman Mao. Miles Davis. The Three Stooges. Salvador Dali. The London AEC Routemaster bus.

Image credits: Egon Steiner, Thilo Parg, Anefo, B.J.Smur, Airwolfhound, GPS56, Ingo Hoehn, William P.Gottlieb, Marco Maas, Egon Steiner, Catch 21 Productions, James Emery, Alan Light, Warren K.Leffler, Rex Gray, Bernard Safran, Jacobs Shore, Steve Nuccia, Thomas the Tank Shop, Flip Chip, R.S. Croes, Thomas J.O'Halloran, German Federal Archives, *World Telegraph and Sun*, Georg Denda, Gage Skidmore, Phil Stanziola, Library of Congress, Caligvala, Florida SuperCon, EMDX, Frantogian, Bltboy, Thilo Parg, GDC Graphics, Goebel, Bill Ingals, D.J. Naquin, National Archives UK, De Factor, Alterna 2, Georges Biard, Mark Brown.

ISBN-13: 978-1727363913
ISBN-10: 1727363914

Published by Montpelier Publishing, London.
Printed and distributed by Amazon Createspace.

Events of
1959

The cast of *Bonanza*, 1959

JANUARY 1959

Thursday 1: Cuba's President Batista flees to the Dominican Republic as the forces of Fidel Castro close in; US navy ships are sent to Cuba to evacuate Americans.

Friday 2: The USSR launches the Luna 1 satellite, the first man made object to escape earth's orbit.

Saturday 3: Alaska is proclaimed the 49th state of the USA by President Dwight D.Eisenhower.

Sunday 4: Luna 1 enters into orbit around the sun, making it the solar system's first artificial planet.

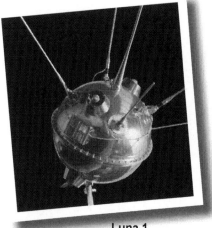

Luna 1

President Eisenhower (seated) signs the Alaska Statehood Act, watched by Vice President Richard Nixon (left), in 1958.

JANUARY 1959

Monday 5: Four British aeronauts from the balloon *Small World* are rescued at sea 19 days after attempting to cross the Atlantic.

Tuesday 6: In Virginia, Mildred and Richard Loving are found guilty of violating state law against inter-racial marriage (miscegenation). The Lovings later take the case to the US Supreme Court where the law is ruled unconstitutional.

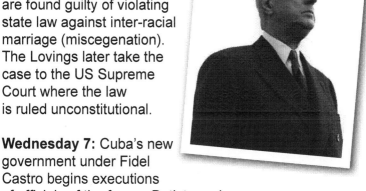

De Gaulle

Wednesday 7: Cuba's new government under Fidel Castro begins executions of officials of the former Batista regime.

Thursday 8: Charles de Gaulle is inaugurated as President of France, the first under the new constitution of the Fifth Republic.

Friday 9: 144 people are killed when a dam bursts at Lago de Sanabria in Zamora, Spain, flooding the nearby village of Ribadelago.

Saturday 10: A federal court in Little Rock, Arkansas, orders the town's school board to begin the process of racial integration of pupils.

Sunday 11: Film actress Claire Delmar, who appeared with Al Jolson in the first 'talkie', *The Jazz Singer* (1927) is found stabbed to death in her home in Carmel, California; her assailant is never identified.

JANUARY 1959

Monday 12: Five boys discover the Caves of Nerja in Spain. Sealed for over 3000 years, the caves are found to be full of paleolithic artefacts.

Tuesday 13: 74 people are killed when the tanker *Mirador* explodes in Iskenderun Harbour in Turkey.

Wednesday 14: Japanese explorers in the Antarctic are shocked to find alive two husky dogs that they had abandoned 11 months earlier; the incident inspires the 2006 Disney film *Eight Below.*

Thursday 15: US officials overturn a Yugoslavian request for the extradition of Andrija Artukovic, wanted for war crimes alleged to have been carried out in Croatia between 1941 and 1942. He is eventually extradited in 1986.

Friday 16: Singer Sade (Helen Folasade Adu) is born in Ibadan, Nigeria.

Saturday 17: The North American Rugby Football League is formed in San Francisco, but the sport fails to catch on.

Sunday 18: 25 people are killed when an Aeroflot Ilyushin IL-14P aircraft crashes at Stalingrad in the USSR.

Sade

JANUARY 1959

Monday 19: Sgt Richard G Corden of the US Army, captured during the Korean War, returns to the USA after eight years in communist China.

Tuesday 20: Soviet Foreign Minister Anastas Mikoyan returns to Moscow after a controversial 17 day tour of the United States.

Wednesday 21: The European Court of Human Rights is established in Strasbourg, France.

Thursday 22: 12 miners are killed during a flood at the River Slope Mine in Port Griffith, Pennsylvania.

Friday 23: US Postmaster General Arthur E. Summerfield announces his proposals for testing 'missile mail'; post sent over long distances by rocket. The idea never catches on.

Saturday 24: Mr Walter Stolle of Essex, England, begins what becomes the longest bicycle tour on record, visiting 159 countries in 18 years.

Sunday 25: The first American passenger jet service begins, running from Los Angeles to New York City in four hours.

Envelope for 'missile mail'.

JANUARY/FEBRUARY 1959

Monday 26: Hearings open in Congress on a bill to admit Hawaii as the 50th state of the USA.

Tuesday 27: The 21st Congress of the Communist Party of the Soviet Union opens in Moscow, with leaders from 70 nations under the chairmanship of Russian premier Nikita Kruschev.

Wednesday 28: Actress Audrey Hepburn receives serious back injuries when she is thrown from a horse in Mexico during the filming of *Unforgiven.*

Thursday 29: Disney releases its animated feature *Sleeping Beauty.* It is the last Disney cartoon in the fairytale genre until *The Little Mermaid* (1989).

Friday 30: 95 people are killed when the Danish ship MS *Hans Hedtoft* sinks off the coast of Greenland.

Saturday 31: The Virginia General Assembly ends its attempts to block racial integration in state schools. Schools had been closed since the previous September in order to avoid compulsory desegregation.

Sunday 1: Male voters in Switzerland vote against female suffrage, which is not granted until 1971.

Audrey Hepburn

FEBRUARY 1959

Monday 2: Schools in Norfolk and Arlington counties in Virginia begin peaceful racial integration.

Buddy Holly

Tuesday 3: 'The Day the Music Died': Buddy Holly, Ritchie Valens and J.P. Richardson (the 'Big Bopper') are killed in a plane crash en route to Fargo, North Dakota. The tragedy is later immortalised in the 1971 Don McLean Song, *American Pie.*

Wednesday 4: Latvian skater Nikolay Shtelbaums sets the world record for the 10,000 metre skate at 16:31.4.

Thursday 5: Soviet Premier Nikita Khrushchev invites US President Dwight D. Eisenhower to visit Moscow and urges him to end the Cold War.

Friday 6: Jack Kilby of Texas Instruments files a patent for the first integrated electronic circuit or 'chip'. Kilby went on to receive the Noble Prize in physics in 2000.

Saturday 7: John Cook and Bob Timm break the world record for the longest continuous flight: 64 days, 22 hours and 21 minutes in a Cessna 172 light aircraft using mid-air refueling to stay aloft.

Sunday 8: One of the original founders of the CIA (Central Intelligence Agency) William J.Donovan, dies aged 76. President Eisenhower remarks 'we have lost the last hero!'

FEBRUARY 1959

Monday 9: The first intercontinental ballistic missile (ICBM) becomes operational in the USSR, beginning a new era in the nuclear arms race.

Tuesday 10: 21 people killed when a tornado hits St Louis, Missouri.

Wednesday 11: The prime ministers of Greece and Turkey sign an agreement on the joint rule of Cyprus following the announcement of the island's independence from Great Britain.

The B-36 bomber

Thursday 12: The USAF decommissions the last of its 1940s B-36 heavy bomber planes, the widest-winged combat aircraft ever built.

Friday 13: Fidel Castro officially replaces Jose Miro Cardona as Prime Minister of Cuba.

Saturday 14: The United States weather bureau releases a report that suggests man-made global warming is occurring, possibly caused by a build up of carbon dioxide.

Sunday 15: Police in New York City make the second largest drugs raid in US history to that date, arresting 27 people and seizing heroin worth $3.6m.

FEBRUARY 1959

Monday 16: US tennis star John McEnroe *(right)* born in Wiesbaden, West Germany.

Tuesday 17: *Vanguard 2,* the first weather satellite, is launched from Cape Canaveral to measure cloud cover for the US Navy.

Wednesday 18: Elections are held in Nepal for the first time in history.

Thursday 19: In London, representatives of Greece, Turkey and the UK sign the treaty of independence for Cyprus, granting each state the right to intervene military to uphold the island's new constitution.

Friday 20: Author and womens' suffrage campaigner Laurence Houseman dies aged 84.

Saturday 21: *The Ben Hecht Show* on US TV is cancelled permanently after guest Salvador Dali uses the word 'orgasm' live on air.

Sunday 22: The USA announces its X-15 'spaceplane' programme to make manned flights into near space (above 50 miles in altitude).

Salvador Dali

FEBRUARY/MARCH 1959

Monday 23: The Prime Minister of Luxembourg, Pierre Frieden, dies in office aged 66.

Tuesday 24: In a bout at London's Wembley Stadium Welsh boxer Joe Erskine defeats future world light heavyweight champion Willie Pastrano.

Wednesday 25: Norway signs an agreement to provide deuterium oxide (heavy water), a key requirement for Israel's nuclear programme.

Thursday 26: The Prime Minister of Rhodesia, Edgar Whitehead, declares a state of emergency following civil unrest.

Friday 27: The wreckage of the USAF B-24 bomber *Lady Be Good*, which crashed in 1943, is found in the Libyan desert. The bodies of the crew, who died from thirst, are not located until February 1960.

Saturday 28: The first of the top secret Project Corona spy satellites, *Discoverer 1*, is launched from Vandenberg Air Force Base in California. The first satellite to have a pole-to-pole orbit, it crash lands somewhere near the South Pole.

Sunday 1: Political and religious leader Archbishop Makarios III returns to Cyprus following the lifting of a travel ban by the British authorities.

Archbishop Makarios III

MARCH 1959

Monday 2: Legendary jazz trumpeter Miles Davis begins recording the album *Kind of Blue*.

Tuesday 3: Comedian Lou Costello, partner of Bud Abbott, dies aged 52.

Miles Davis

Wednesday 4: *Pioneer IV* becomes the first US spacecraft to exit Earth's orbit (after the USSR's *Lunik*).

Thursday 5: In Ankara, the USA signs a treaty to defend Iran, Turkey and Pakistan in case of attack.

Friday 6: The Castro government orders all rents in Cuba to be reduced by fifty percent.

Saturday 7: In an article in the *Saturday Evening Post*, US Secretary of State Dean Acheson warns that Allied troops should no longer hold West Berlin.

Sunday 8: Comedy group the Marx Brothers make their final screen appearance in *The Incredible Jewel Robbery* on CBS TV.

Lou Costello

MARCH 1959

Monday 9: Mattel Inc launches the Barbie doll, named after the daughter of its inventor, Ruth Handler.

Tuesday 10: 30,000 Tibetans surround Norbulingka Palace, home of the Dalai Lama, to prevent his arrest by Chinese authorities.

Wednesday 11: The Sikorsky SH-3 *Sea King* helicopter makes its first test flight. The first amphibious helicopter, it is still in use with many air-sea rescue services.

Thursday 12: The US House of Representatives votes to allow Hawaii to become the 50th state of the USA.

Friday 13: US flag manufacturers ask that the adoption of the 50 star flag be postponed until July 1960 due to the backlog created by the adoption of the 49 star flag after the admission of Alaska to the Union in January.

Saturday 14: Sharaf Rashidov is elected de facto ruler of Uzbekistan, remaining in power until his death in 1983.

Sunday 15: Canadian Robert Foster sets the world record for holding the breath underwater (13m:42.5), which remains unbroken until 2007.

Prototype
Sikorsky SH-3 Sea
King helicopter

MARCH 1959

Monday 16: US rapper Flavor Flav (William Jonathan Drayton Jr) is born in Roosevelt, New York.

Tuesday 17: To avoid arrest by the Chinese authorities, Tenzin Gyatso, the 14th Dalai Lama, flees Tibet and receives sanctuary in India.

The 14th Dalai Lama

Wednesday 18: Film director Luc Besson (*The Fifth Element*) born in Paris, France.

Luc Besson

Thursday 19: Fighting breaks out in Lhasa between Tibetans and Chinese troops.

Friday 20: The world record for the most number of people in a phone box is set in Modesto, California, as 32 college students squeeze into a 7' tall, 32" square booth.

Saturday 21: Pope John XXIII orders that Jews are no longer to be described as 'faithless' in the Roman Catholic church's prayers for their conversion.

Sunday 22: In a televised address, Cuban dictator Fidel Castro announces that all racial segregation in Cuba will be outlawed.

MARCH 1959

Monday 23: Nine miners are killed in an explosion at Brimstone, Tennessee.

Tuesday 24: New York City Council officials introduce a proposal for New York City to become a state in its own right.

Wednesday 25: In his first presidential press conference, Charles De Gaulle states that France supports German reunification provided they do not expand their border.

Raymond Chandler

Thursday 26: Anglo-American author Raymond Chandler, creator of fictional detective Philip Marlowe (who appeared in novels including *The Big Sleep* and *Farewell, My Lovely,*) dies aged 70.

Friday 27: North Carolina becomes the first US state to introduce compulsory polio vaccination for all children.

Saturday 28: The government of Tibet is abolished by the Chinese, and the Dalai Lama replaced by a puppet ruler, the Panchen Lama.

Sunday 29: Barthélemy Boganda, the first Prime Minister of the Central African Republic, is killed in plane crash near the capital, Bangui.

Stamp showing Barthélemy Boganda

MARCH/APRIL 1959

Monday 30: A senior judge in Japan rules that American military occupation of the country is unconstitutional; the decision is later reversed.

Tuesday 31: The Dalai Lama begins permanent exile with his government in the former British hill station of Dharamsala in the Indian state of Himachal Pradesh, where he remains to this day.

David Hyde Pierce

Wednesday 1: A USAF cargo plane crashes at Orting, Washington, killing all four on board. The incident becomes the focus of UFOlogists and conspiracy theorists after witnesses describe the aircraft hitting an unidentified object before it crashed.

Thursday 2: NASA announces the names of seven men chosen as astronauts for Project Mercury, the first US manned space programme.

Friday 3: Actor David Hyde Pierce (Dr Niles Crane in *Frasier*) is born in Saratoga Springs, New York.

Saturday 4: US President Dwight D. Eisenhower announces his country's commitment to keeping South Vietnam as a non-communist state separate from North Vietnam.

Sunday 5: In Dortmund, West Germany, Rong Guotan becomes the first Chinese player to win the World Table Tennis Championships.

APRIL 1959

Monday 6: *Gigi* wins a record nine Oscars at the Academy Awards, including Best Picture.

Tuesday 7: The Israeli parliament institutes the first Holocaust Memorial Day.

Wednesday 8: Martin Luther King addresses a crowd of 26,000 high school pupils and college students in Washington on the Youth March for Integrated Schools.

Thursday 9: Legendary American architect Frank Lloyd Wright dies aged 91.

Friday 10: In Maryland, convicted murderer Leonard Shockley, 17, becomes the last juvenile to be executed in the United States.

Saturday 11: William H. Pickering, director of the Jet Propulsion Laboratory declares that the USA will put a man on the moon within 5 to 10 years.

New York's Guggenheim Museum, designed by Frank Lloyd Wright

Sunday 12: In a speech in Indianapolis, Indiana, Senator John F. Kennedy makes the famous quote, 'When written in Chinese, the word crisis is composed of two characters; one represents danger and the other represents opportunity.' It is later shown to be an incorrect translation.

APRIL 1959

Monday 13: Singer and actor Mario Lanza gives his final concert in Kiel, West Germany.

Tuesday 14: The long range *Atlas D* intercontinental ballistic missile is tested, unsuccessfully, at Cape Canaveral.

Wednesday 15: Actress Emma Thompson (of the *Harry Potter* and *Nanny McPhee* film series) is born in London.

Sean Bean

Thursday 16: The first *Thor* nuclear missiles become operational in the UK under the Royal Air Force.

Friday 17: Actor Sean Bean (*Sharpe, Game of Thrones*) is born in Sheffield, Yorkshire.

Saturday 18: The Corvette Stingray concept sports car makes its debut at Marlboro Raceway, Maryland, USA.

Sunday 19: Mrs Ida Pidoux of Oulens-sur-Lucens becomes the first woman in Switzerland to vote, following the introduction of female suffrage in local elections.

The Corvette Stingray

APRIL 1959

Monday 20: Aeroflot's *Illyushin II-18* propellor airliner goes into service. Widely used all over the world, it is still in service today.

Tuesday 21: Mr Alfred Dean sets the world record for catching the largest ever fish on a rod: a 2664 pound great white shark off the coast at Ceduna, South Australia.

Wednesday 22: US crime drama *The Untouchables* premieres on CBS TV.

Thursday 23: Panamanian authorities accuse actor John Wayne of financing a coup in the country; he dismisses the charges as ridiculous.

Friday 24: Champion US racehorse Omaha, who won the Triple Crown in 1935, dies aged 27.

Saturday 25: The US-Canadian 370-mile St Lawrence Seaway ship navigation opens, linking the Atlantic Ocean with Lake Superior.

Sunday 26: John Corabi, guitarist with heavy metal group Mötley Crüe is born in Philadelphia.

The St Lawrence Seaway

APRIL/MAY 1959

Monday 27: Pop singer Sheena Easton (*Modern Girl* and *Morning Train*) born in Bellshill, North Lanarkshire.

Tuesday 28: In a speech at Columbia University, former US President Harry S Truman states that he made the decision to drop atomic bombs on Japan in order to avoid a greater loss of life through invasion.

Sheena Easton

Wednesday 29: 28 people, including European gymnastics champion Joaquín Blume, are killed when an Iberia Airlines DC-3 aeroplane crashes near Cuenca, Spain.

Thursday 30: Stephen Harper, 22nd Prime Minister of Canada (2006-2015) is born in Toronto.

Friday 1: The presidents of Ghana and Guinea announce the merger of their nations into a Union of African States, which lasts until 1961.

Saturday 2: Racing driver Jerry Unser Jr is fatally injured while practicing for the Indianapolis 500. His death leads to the introduction of compulsory fireproof suits for drivers.

Sunday 3: Comedian and writer Ben Elton (*The Young Ones, Blackadder*) is born in Catford, south London.

Ben Elton

MAY 1959

Monday 4: The first Gramophone ('Grammy') Awards are held in Beverley Hills. Domenico Modugno's *Volare* wins Song of the Year, and Perry Como's *Catch a Falling Star* is Best Male Vocal Performance.

Tuesday 5: The USA and West Germany sign an agreement to train German personnel in the operation of nuclear weapons.

Perry Como

Wednesday 6: South Vietnam introduces the death penalty for anyone taking part in the communist Viet Cong insurgency.

Thursday 7: At Cambridge University, scientist and novelist C.P. Snow warns in his Rede Lecture 'The Two Cultures' at Cambridge University of the growing rift between science and humanities and the problems this poses for western civilization.

Friday 8: The first Little Caesars pizza restaurant opens in Garden City, Michigan. The company goes on to become the third largest pizza chain in the USA.

Saturday 9: Eritrea enters into federal union with neighbouring Ethiopia, which lasts for ten years during which Mali is added as another member state.

Sunday 10: Azef Youssef Atta is enthroned in Alexandria, Egypt as Pope Cyril VI of the Coptic Orthodox Church, remaining its spiritual leader until 1971.

MAY 1959

Monday 11: Foreign ministers of Britain, France and the USSR meet in Geneva for a 17 day conference on German reunification; no agreement is made.

Tuesday 12: Hours after his divorce from Debbie Reynolds become final, Eddie Fisher marries Elizabeth Taylor in Los Angeles.

Eddie Fisher

Wednesday 13: Brazil beats England 2:0 during an end of season soccer tour of South America.

Thursday 14: For the first time, radio signals are bounced off the moon, with a transmission sent from Britain to the USA.

Elizabeth Taylor

Friday 15: Fidel Castro announces an end to the war crimes trials conducted since his takeover of Cuba in January, during which several hundred people were executed.

Saturday 16: Following Indo-Chinese border tensions after the Tibetan uprising, the Chinese Ambassador to India announces that Tibet is an 'inalienable part of China's territory'.

Sunday 17: Placido Domingo makes his operatic debut as Matteo Borsa in *Rigoletto*.

MAY 1959

Monday 18: Just hours after his divorce to Elaine Davis is finalised, actor Mickey Rooney marries his fifth wife, Barbara Ann Thomson.

Morrissey

Tuesday 19: North Vietnam begins building the 'Ho Chi Minh Trail', the supply line for the invasion of South Vietnam.

Wednesday 20: The US Justice Department restores the citizenship of 4978 Japanese-Americans who renounced it during the Second World War.

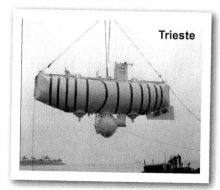

Trieste

Thursday 21: The Swiss-Italian deep-sea submersible *Trieste* makes its first test dive, to 700 feet (213m). In 1960 she descends to the bottom of the Mariana Trench, the deepest known spot in the world's oceans.

Friday 22: Singer and activist Morrissey is born at Davyhulme, Lancashire.

Saturday 23: Civil war breaks out in Laos, south east Asia, between communists and monarchists. It lasts until a communist victory in December 1975.

Sunday 24: British Empire Day is renamed Commonwealth Day.

MAY 1959

Monday 25: US mass murderer Charles Starkweather is granted a dramatic last minute reprieve shortly before his execution. He eventually goes to the electric chair on 25 June.

Tuesday 26: The 1964 Olympic Games are awarded to Tokyo.

Wednesday 27: The funeral takes place in Washington of US Secretary of State John Foster Dulles who died on 22 April.

Thursday 28: The Mermaid Theatre opens in the City of London, the first to be built there since the time of Shakespeare.

Friday 29: American, British, French and Russian representatives negotiate the future of Berlin during a transatlantic flight, in what the press reports as 'the first international conference in the clouds'.

Saturday 30: The 3348 ft/1020 metre long Auckland Harbour Bridge *(left)* opens in New Zealand.

Sunday 31: The Calvin Jubilee: representatives of Reformed churches from around the world gather in Geneva to mark the 450th anniversary of the birth of the reformer John Calvin.

JUNE 1959

Monday 1: Author Sax Rohmer (Arthur Henry Ward) creator of arch-villain Fu Manchu, dies aged 76.

Tuesday 2: Twelve people are killed in Schuylkill Haven, Pennsylvania, when a truck carrying propane explodes.

The Three Stooges

Wednesday 3: The British colony of Singapore is granted semi-autonomous status within the Commonwealth.

Thursday 4: The 190th and final Three Stooges comedy short, *Sappy Bull Fighters*, is released in cinemas.

Friday 5: Soviet navy commander Nikolay Artamonov defects to the USA. He is recaptured by Soviet agents in 1975.

Saturday 6: The first 'satellite' communication between world leaders is made as President Eisenhower sends a radio message which is bounced off the moon to Canada's prime minister, John Diefenbaker.

Sunday 7: US Vice President Mike Pence born in Columbus, Indiana.

Vice President Pence

JUNE 1959

Monday 8: The US postal service makes its first 'missile mail' delivery of 3000 letters fired in a Regulus 1 rocket from Norfolk, Virginia to Mayport, Florida.

Tuesday 9: The first submarine able to launch ballistic missiles, the USS *George Washington (right)* is launched.

Wednesday 10: Soviet premier Nikita Khruschev issues an ultimatum for occupying US, British and French troops to be withdrawn from West Berlin by 10 June 1960.

Thursday 11: Actor and comedian Hugh Laurie (Dr Gregory House in *House*) is born in Oxford, England.

Friday 12: Construction begins on HMS *Dreadnought*, the first British nuclear submarine.

Saturday 13: Seven people are killed when police in Angamaly, Kerala, India, open fire on a crowd protesting against the elected communist state government.

Hugh Laurie

Sunday 14: Dominican exiles, aided by Fidel Castro, unsuccessfully attempt to invade the Dominican Republic to overthrow the government of Rafael Leónidas Trujillo.

JUNE 1959

Monday 15: A US Navy patrol plane is attacked by two MiG-15 fighters near North Korea.

Tuesday 16: Actor George Reeves, famous for playing Superman in the original TV series, is found shot dead in his Beverly Hills home after apparently committing suicide.

Wednesday 17: Flamboyant pianist Liberace is awarded $22,400 in his libel suit against Britain's *Daily Mirror*, in which he had been described as a homosexual.

Thursday 18: HM Queen Elizabeth II arrives in Canada to begin a 45 day tour, the longest stay in the country by a Canadian monarch.

George Reeves

Friday 19: US Defence Secretary Neil H. McElroy approves a new air defence master plan, ordering new missiles to keep up with those being developed by the USSR.

Saturday 20: The Soviet Union reverses plans made in 1957 to provide China with an atomic bomb, and refuses to provide any further assistance.

Sunday 21: Winnipeg in Canada becomes the first city in north America to adopt a single emergency services telephone number (999).

Liberace

JUNE 1959

Monday 22: The first multinational treaty on nuclear security comes into force, signed by the nations of western Europe, the USA and Canada.

Tuesday 23: Seán Lemass replaces Éamon de Valera as Prime Minister of the Republic of Ireland, and begins a policy of cooperation rather than unification with Ulster.

Wednesday 24: Musical film *Porgy and Bess* starring Sidney Poitier and Dorothy Dandridge is released.

Thursday 25: Charles Starkweather, who murdered 11 people in 1958, is executed at Nebraska State Penitentiary.

Friday 26: Ingemar Johansson of Sweden becomes the world heavyweight boxing champion after knocking out Floyd Patterson at Yankee Stadium.

Johansson KOs Patterson

Saturday 27: Voters in Hawaii go to the polls to approve the decision to become the 50th state of the USA, with the vast majority in favour.

Sunday 28: 49 year old Haitian immigrant Ardouin Antonio dies in New York of a mystery illness. Preserved tissue samples later suggest his was one of the earliest known cases of HIV/AIDS.

JUNE/JULY 1959

Monday 29: Pope John XXIII issues his first encyclical, *Ad Petri Cathedram,* calling for renewal in the Roman Catholic Church.

Tuesday 30: 21 pupils are killed when a USAF F-100 plane crashes into an elementary school in Ishikawa, Okinawa, Japan.

Wednesday 1: The USA, Britain and several Commonwealth countries adopt a new international standard for the yard (0.9144m) and the pound (0.45kg).

Pope John XXIII

Thursday 2: A fire at the Pentagon destroys $30m worth of computer equipment.

Friday 3: Wimbledon is won for the first time by a South American, as Alex Olmedo of Peru beats Rod Laver in the men's singles final.

Saturday 4: The 49th star is officially added to the American flag on the first Fourth of July following Alaska's admission to the Union.

Sunday 5: The Saarland region of Germany, under French occupation since the end of the Second World War, is formally handed back to West Germany at the end of a transitional process begun in 1957.

JULY 1959

Monday 6: A cargo plane carrying nuclear weapons crashes on takeoff from Barksdale Air Force base in Louisiana; safety devices prevent the payload from detonating.

Tuesday 7: Venus passes between Earth and the star Regulus at 14.28 GMT, an event which will not occur again until 2044. The dimming of the starlight enables astronomers to make calculations about the Venusian atmosphere.

Wednesday 8: Major Dale R. Buis and M/Sgt Chester M. Ovnand become the first Americans to die in the Vietnam War, hit by a Viet Cong attack while advising the South Vietnam military.

Thursday 9: Controversial clergyman and civil rights campaigner Al Sharpton preaches his first sermon at a church in Brooklyn, NY, aged just four.

Friday 10: A memorial to Major Frank Foley CMG (1884-1958) is dedicated in Harel, Israel, for his role in helping Jewish families escape Berlin in WW2 via the British Embassy.

Frank Foley

Saturday 11: Singer-songwriter Suzanne Vega (*Tom's Diner*) born in Santa Monica, California.

Sunday 12: Over 100 people are killed in Honduras during a failed attempt to oust President Ramon Villeda Morales.

JULY 1959

Monday 13: America's worst nuclear accident occurrs as the nuclear reactor at Santa Susana Feld Laboratory in California goes into meltdown.

Tuesday 14: 30 people are killed in the 'Kirkuk Massacre', in Kirkuk, Iraq as fighting breaks out between ethnic Turks and Kurds.

Juno II rocket in flames

Wednesday 15: The largest strike in US history beings as 500,000 steelworkers down tools; the walkout lasts for 116 days.

Thursday 16: Seconds after launching at Cape Canaveral, a Juno II rocket veers off course to central Florida, and has to be remotely destroyed by ground control.

Friday 17: Jazz singing legend Billie Holiday dies in New York aged 44 following a battle with drug addiction.

Saturday 18: Osvaldo Dorticos Torrado is sworn in as President of Cuba. His predecessor, Manuel Urrutia, flees the country after disagreeing with Fidel Castro over reforms.

Sunday 19: The leaders of Liberia, Guinea and Ghana form an economic and political grouping which later becomes the Organisation of African Unity.

JULY 1959

Monday 20: Fleet Admiral William D. Leahy, highest ranking US naval officer during the Second World War, dies aged 84.

Tuesday 21: US federal judge Frederick van Pelt rules that D.H.Lawrence's novel *Lady Chatterley's Lover* is not obscene and is fit for publication.

Wednesday 22: The Japan-Paraguay Immigration Agreement is signed, providing for 85,000 Japanese to emigrate to Paraguay. Eventually only around 8000 make the move.

Thursday 23: Actor James Stewart (*It's a Wonderful Life*) is promoted to the rank of Brigadier General in the US Air Force Reserves.

Friday 24: Soviet premier Nikita Khrushchev and US Vice-President Richard Nixon debate the merits of capitalism versus communism at an American home improvement show in Moscow.

Saturday 25: On the 50th anniversary of the first aeroplane flight across the English Channel, the futuristic British SR N1 'hovercraft' makes the same journey.

SR N1 hovercraft

Sunday 26: Actor and director Kevin Spacey born in South Orange, New Jersey.

JULY/AUGUST 1959

Monday 27: In a passionate speech in Parliament, British politician Enoch Powell attacks the government for attempting to cover up a massacre of Mau-Mau suspects at Hola Camp in Kenya.

The UN Medal

IN THE SERVICE OF PEACE

Tuesday 28: Lt Col William Rankin of the USAF becomes the only pilot known to have bailed out of a plane into a thunderstorm and survived.

Wednesday 29: The Legitimacy Act 1959 receives Royal Assent, giving equal rights to children born out of wedlock in Britain.

Thursday 30: The United Nations Medal is introduced for those serving with UN forces.

Friday 31: The Basque separatist organisation ETA (*Euzkadi Ta Askatasuna*) is founded in Spain; it goes on to kill more than 800 people in terrorist attacks.

Saturday 1: Georges Vanier becomes the first French-Canadian to serve as Governor-General of Canada.

Sunday 2: 16 people killed as rioting breaks out in Temirtau, Kazakhstan over bad conditions for workers on a Soviet industrialisation project.

AUGUST 1959

Monday 3: At least 50 people are killed during pro-independence rioting in the colony of Portuguese Guinea.

Tuesday 4: The US government pays almost £100m to the government of the Philippines for war damages and the devaluation of its currency when under US rule. Other claims of up to $950m are rejected.

Wednesday 5: Three months of negotiations between the US, USSR, UK and France over the occupation of West Berlin end with no resolution.

Thursday 6: The legendary USAF wartime bomber plane, the B-17 Flying Fortress, first flown in 1935, is used for the last time militarily, as a remote controlled target for air-to-air missiles.

The B-17 Flying Fortress

Friday 7: The United Nations reports a deficit of over $7m after 60 nations lag behind in annual payments.

Saturday 8: After more than 1000 performances in the London musical *My Fair Lady,* Julie Andrews retires from the role of Eliza Doolittle. She is replaced by Anne Rogers.

Sunday 9: The USA's first intercontinental ballistic missile (ICBM), the SM-65 *Atlas*, is declared operational.

AUGUST 1959

Monday 10: Actress Rosanna Arquette (*Desperately Seeking Susan, Pulp Fiction*) is born in New York City.

Rosana Arquette

Tuesday 11: The longest home run of all time was hit in a minor league baseball game in Carlbad, New Mexico. The ball was not found until the next day, 733 feet outside the stadium.

Wednesday 12: High schools in Little Rock, Arkansas, reopen a year after being closed in order to avoid racial integration of pupils.

Thursday 13: North Korea and Japan agree on terms for the repatriation of Koreans in Japan.

Friday 14: The first photograph of the earth is taken by an orbiting satellite, Explorer 6, demonstrating the potential of observing weather from space.

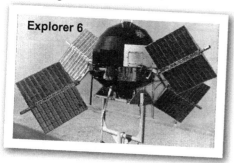
Explorer 6

Saturday 15: The first fatal crash involving a passenger jet plane takes place when a Boeing 707 training flight crashes at Calverton, NY.

Sunday 16: The first TV broadcasts begin in Queensland, Australia, as Channel 9 goes on the air in Brisbane. TV was first broadcast in Sydney and Melbourne in 1956.

AUGUST 1959

Monday 17: 28 people are killed when an earthquake, 7.1 on the Richter Scale, strikes the Madison River Canyon in Montana.

Tuesday 18: The Inter American Commission on Human Rights is signed by 21 member countries of the Organisation of American States based throughout north and south America.

Wednesday 19: Anglo-American sculptor Jacob Epstein dies aged 78. One of his last works was *St Michael's Victory over the Devil* (1958, *right*) at Coventry Cathedral.

Thursday 20: Over 100 people are drowned when the ferry *Pilar II* capsizes off the coast of Palawan Island in the Philippines.

Friday 21: Hawaii is proclaimed the 50th state of the USA, with William F.Quinn as the first state governor.

Saturday 22: The New York Philharmonic Orchestra gives its first performance in the USSR, playing Shostakovich's Fifth Symphony in Moscow in the presence of the composer.

Sunday 23: The last baseball game is played at Ebbet's Field in Brooklyn, the historic home of the Brooklyn Dodgers before the team's move to Los Angeles.

AUGUST 1959

Monday 24: House of Fraser takes over Harrod's department store in London, in a £37m deal.

The launch of the Mini

Tuesday 25: Indian and Chinese troops clash for the first time in a border dispute along the McMahon Line at Longju.

Wednesday 26: The British Motor Corporation launches the Mini, a highly economical compact family car. Designed by Sir Alec Issigonis, it becomes a global success and remains in production until 2000.

Thursday 27: The Polaris missile is successfully launched for the first time, from the US navy submarine Observation Island.

Friday 28: The first mass uprising by communist rebels begins in South Vietnam.

Saturday 29: John Lennon and Paul McCartney (of The Quarrymen) and George Harrison (of The Les Stewart Quartet) play together for the first time at the Casbah Coffee Club in Liverpool.

Sunday 30: The Pan-Somali Movement is formed in Mogadishu, with the aim of uniting the disparate Somali people into one African nation.

AUGUST/SEPTEMBER 1959

Harold MacMillan

Monday 31: British Prime Minister Harold Macmillan and US President Dwight Eisenhower make a joint TV broadcast from 10, Downing Street.

Tuesday 1: At least seven people are killed when police fire on a crowd during food riots in Calcutta, India.

Wednesday 2: Norwegian missionary and student of Tibetan culture, Theo Sorensen, dies aged 86.

Thursday 3: Singapore replaces the Union Flag and God *Save the Queen* with its own flag and anthem as part of its move towards independence from the UK, achieved in 1965.

Friday 4: The highly influential American National Exhibition in Moscow closes after six weeks.

Saturday 5: The Kingdom of Laos declares a state of emergency following incursions of communist rebels from North Vietnam.

Sunday 6: The first jet airline service from the USA to Honolulu, Hawaii begins, enabling the islands to become a premier tourist destination.

SEPTEMBER 1959

Monday 7: 81 students depart from Kenya to the USA and Canada on the 'Kennedy Airlift', a scholarship scheme sponsored by Senator John F. Kennedy.

Tuesday 8: The USA enacts a law to protect mustangs and other wild horses from being hunted.

Wednesday 9: Tests using an Atlas-D missile fired from Cape Canaveral prove that heat shields could protect humans during re-entry from space.

Thursday 10: Francis Joseph Huchet, the last man to be hanged in the Channel Islands, is sentenced to death in St Helier, Jersey.

Pernell Roberts as Adam Cartwright in *Bonanza*

Friday 11: Children's cartoon series *Noggin the Nog*, created by Oliver Postgate and Peter Firmin, is first broadcast on the BBC.

Saturday 12: US western series *Bonanza* is first broadcast on NBC. The first western to be televised in colour, it runs for 440 episodes.

Sunday 13: The first man-made object lands on the Moon as the Soviet Lunik 2 satellite crash-lands near the Sea of Tranquility.

SEPTEMBER 1959

Monday 14: Morten Harket, lead singer of A-Ha, is born in Kongsberg, Norway.

Tuesday 15: Soviet leader Nikita Khrushchev arrives for an 11 day visit to the United States.

Wednesday 16: French President Charles de Gaulle announces that after five years of war and more than 21,000 French troops killed, 'self determination' for the colony of Algeria is inevitable.

Thursday 17: Transit 1A, the first navigational satellite, is launched from Cape Canaveral, but fails to reach orbit. Later attempts are successful, enabling a prototype GPS navigation system to be set up in the early 1960s.

Friday 18: 47 miners die as the result of a fire at Auchengeich Colliery, Lanarkshire, Scotland.

Auchengeich Colliery Memorial, Lanarkshire

Saturday 19: During his US visit, Nikita Khruschev announces his annoyance at being barred from Disneyland due to security concerns.

Sunday 20: 19 senior Iraqi army officers are executed for their role in an uprising in March 1959.

SEPTEMBER 1959

Monday 21: Ford launches the Ford Falcon. TV adverts for the car feature the first animated versions of Charles M.Schulz's *Peanuts* cartoon characters.

Ford Falcon

Tuesday 22: The USS *Patrick Henry,* the second American ballistic missile submarine, is launched in Groton, Connecticut.

Wednesday 23: American comedian Jason Alexander (George Costanza in *Seinfeld*) is born in Newark, New Jersey.

Thursday 24: The US Atlas rocket, on a mission to photograph the dark side of the Moon, explodes on the launch pad.

Jason Alexander

Friday 25: S.W.R.D. Bandaranaike, Prime Minister of the former British colony of Ceylon (now Sri Lanka) is assassinated by a Buddhist priest, Talduwe Somarama.

Saturday 26: Over 5000 people are killed as Typhoon Vera hits Japan, the strongest storm ever recorded in the country's history.

Sunday 27: Nikita Khruschev and Dwight D. Eisenhower hold their final meeting on the last day of Khruschev's tour of the USA.

SEPTEMBER/OCTOBER 1959

Monday 28: The Hanna-Barbera cartoon series *The Quick Draw McGraw Show* is first broadcast on US TV.

Tuesday 29: The British colony of Brunei is granted semi-autonomous protectorate status. It becomes fully independent in 1984.

Chairman Mao

Wednesday 30: Soviet premier Nikita Khrushchev begins talks with China's Chairman Mao in Beijing (Peking).

Thursday 1: Huge celebrations mark the tenth anniversary of the founding of the People's Republic of China.

Friday 2: Paranormal TV series *The Twilight Zone* premieres on CBS TV.

Saturday 3: The ballistic missile submarine USS *Theodore Roosevelt*, named after the 26th President of the USA, is launched by his daughter, Alice Roosevelt Longworth *(left)*.

Sunday 4: The Soviets launch Luna 3, on a mission to photograph the dark side of the Moon.

OCTOBER 1959

Monday 5: The IBM 1401 computer is launched, the first fully transistorised computer for business use. With 1.4KB of memory, it cost $2500 per month to hire.

Tuesday 6: A Congressional subcommittee establishes that popular US TV quiz show *Twenty One* was rigged. The story is later made into the film *Quiz Show* in 1994.

Wednesday 7: The Luna 3 probe takes the first photos of the dark side of the moon and transmits them to Earth.

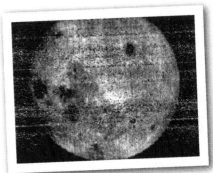

The first picture from Luna 3

Thursday 8: The Conservatives, led by Harold Macmillan, win the General Election in the UK with a 365 seat majority.

Friday 9: The first black military pilot, US-born Eugene Bullard receives the *Légion d'honneur,* France's highest military award, for services to the French Air Force during the First World War.

Saturday 10: Singer-songwriter Kirsty MacColl is born in Croydon, Surrey. (Died 2000).

Eugene Bullard

Sunday 11: Fighting breaks out in the Belgian Congo between rival tribes in the run up to independence.

OCTOBER 1959

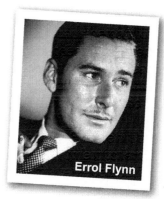

Errol Flynn

Monday 12: Yuri Gagarin, later the first man in space, is selected to be a cosmonaut following evaluation at Murmansk air base.

Tuesday 13: US satellite Explorer 7 is launched, the first to be equipped with instruments to study climate and radiation in the Earth's atmosphere.

Wednesday 14: Swashbuckling film legend Errol Flynn dies aged 50.

Thursday 15: Sarah 'Fergie' Ferguson, Duchess of York and former wife of HRH Prince Andrew, is born in London.

Friday 16: General George C.Marshall, US Secretary of State and originator of the post-war Marshall Plan to aid Europe, dies aged 78.

Sarah Ferguson

Saturday 17: Long running British boy's magazine *The Hotspur,* the last of the illustrated weekly story papers, ceases publication after 1197 issues. It is later relaunched as a comic, *The New Hotspur.*

Sunday 18: For the first time, a former US President (Harry S. Truman) is lampooned on TV (*The Jack Benny Program*), causing controversy among critics and viewers about whether it is appropriate to make fun of a President.

OCTOBER 1959

Monday 19: *The Miracle Worker,* a play about the early life of deaf-blind author Helen Keller, opens on Broadway, starring Anne Bancroft and Patty Duke.

Tuesday 20: The University of Oxford grants its five affiliated women's colleges equal status with men's colleges.

A scene from *The Miracle Worker*

Wednesday 21: New York's Solomon R. Guggenheim Museum opens.

Thursday 22: All contact with the moon probe Luna 3 is lost, leading to speculation that it was burnt up in the Earth's atmosphere.

Friday 23: Following a successful opening in Britain in September, Hammer horror film *The Mummy,* starring Christopher Lee and Peter Cushing, premieres in the USA.

Saturday 24: Cuba nationalises over 150 American investments including hotels, casinos and racetracks, leading to a sharp drop in US tourism.

Sunday 25: The last propellor-driven presidential plane, (Air Force One) makes its final flight before replacement by a jet powered version.

OCTOBER/NOVEMBER 1959

Monday 26: Chrysler launches the Plymouth Valiant at the International Motor Show in London.

Tuesday 27: Over 1000 people are killed in Mexico when a hurricane strikes the states of Colima and Jalisco.

Wednesday 28: DuPont launches the synthetic elastic fabric spandex, under the trade name of Lycra.

Thursday 29: French cartoon legend Asterix the Gaul makes his debut in comic magazine *Pilote*.

Friday 30: Piedmont Airlines Flight 349 crashes near Crozet, Virgina, killing 23 of the 24 persons on board. The lone survivor, Phil Bradley is found 36 hours later.

Saturday 31: Television is seen in Africa for the first time as the Western Nigeria Television Service starts broadcasting.

Sunday 1: White journalist John Howard Griffin of Texas begins darkening his skin with chemicals in order to pass as black, to research his book on racial equality, *Black Like Me.*

The Plymouth Valiant

NOVEMBER 1959

Monday 2: The first section of Britain's M1 motorway is opened between Watford and Rugby.

Tuesday 3: French President Charles de Gaulle announces that France will set up a nuclear strike force, the *Force de frappe.*

Wednesday 4: Six Israeli jets and four Egyptian MiG-17s clash in a dogfight on the Israeli-Egyptian border.

Thursday 5: Singer Bryan Adams is born in Kingston, Ontario.

Friday 6: Boston physician Dr Bernard Lown begins work on developing what later becomes known as a defibrillator.

Bryan Adams

Saturday 7: Chinese premier Zhou Enlai proposes that both Chinese and Indian troops withdraw from the disputed border territory of Ladakh.

Sunday 8: Egypt and the Sudan sign a treaty over mutual use of the River Nile in development projects.

NOVEMBER 1959

Monday 9: The first ski-doo or lightweight snowmobile goes into production in Valcourt, Quebec.

Tuesday 10: The USS *Triton,* at 5000 tons the world's largest submarine at that time, goes into service.

Wednesday 11: London Transport icon the AEC Routemaster bus begins service in London. They remain widely in use until 2005 with one 'heritage' route remaining in 2018.

London's iconic Routemaster bus

Thursday 12: William Morrison, First Viscount Dunrossil is selected to become Governor-General of Australia.

Friday 13: The Narrows Bridge in Perth, Australia, opens. At the time the 1301 ft bridge is the largest to be made of precast concrete.

Saturday 14: Actor Paul McGann (*Dr Who*) born in Liverpool, England.

Paul McGann

Sunday 15: C.T.R Wilson, Nobel Prize winning Scottish physicist and inventor of the Cloud Chamber for detecting radiation, dies aged 90.

NOVEMBER 1959

Monday 16: *The Sound of Music,* written by Rodgers and Hammerstein, premieres on Broadway starring Mary Martin as Maria von Trapp.

Tuesday 17: Brazilian composer Heitor Villa-Lobos, author of over 2000 works, dies aged 72.

Wednesday 18: *Ben Hur,* which goes on to become the most popular film of the year and win 12 Academy Awards, debuts at Loew's Theater in New York.

Thursday 19: In its third unsuccessful year, the Ford motor company ceases production of its futuristic Edsel model, after a loss of $250m and numerous technical problems.

Friday 20: The United Nations passes the Declaration of the Rights of the Child.

Saturday 21: US disc jockey Alan Freed is fired from New York's WABC radio station after refusing to deny that he was bribed to promote certain records, in what becomes known as the 'Payola' scandal.

Sunday 22: Songwriter Sam M.Lewis, author of hits such as *Dinah* and *Has Anybody Seen My Gal?* dies aged 74.

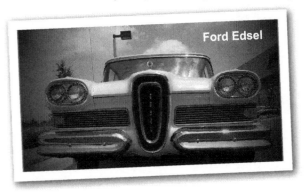
Ford Edsel

NOVEMBER 1959

Monday 23: The Curtiss-Wright corporation announces the development of a new type of engine with only two moving parts, later known as the Wankel rotary engine.

Tuesday 24: The Proton Synchotron, the first particle accelerator to be used by the European nuclear agency CERN for atomic research, goes into operation in Geneva.

Charles Kennedy

Wednesday 25: Scottish politician Charles Kennedy, leader of the Liberal Democrat party from 1999 to 2006, is born in Inverness. (Died 2015).

Thursday 26: The maiden flight of the Atlas-Able rocket, the most powerful built by the USA to that date, ends in failure after a misfire less than a minute after launch.

Friday 27: Rioting takes place in Tokyo as thousands of anti-American demonstrators storm the grounds of the Japanese parliament.

Saturday 28: The first 'Nashville Sit-In' protests against racial segregation in cafes begins at Harvey's Department Store in Nashville, Tennessee.

Sunday 29: Rev Martin Luther King *(right)* makes his final sermon as a Baptist minister in Montgomery, Alabama, resigning to work as a civil rights activist.

NOVEMBER/DECEMBER 1959

Monday 30: János Kádár, communist party leader in Hungary, announces that Soviet troops will stay in the country as long as necessary. They remain until 1991.

János Kádár

Tuesday 1: The Antarctic Treaty, allowing Antarctica to be used for peaceful purposes only, is signed by all 12 nations with bases on the continent.

Wednesday 2: 423 people are killed when a dam at Malpasset, France, collapses, flooding the nearby city of Fréjus.

Albert Lutuli

Thursday 3: US President Dwight D. Eisenhower embarks on a three week 'mission of peace and goodwill' to Europe and the Middle East.

Friday 4: 'Sam', a rhesus monkey, is launched 53 miles into space and then returned to earth to test an emergency escape mechanism.

Saturday 5: Albert Lutuli of the African National Congress issues a statement appealing to the British people to boycott South Africa because of apartheid.

Sunday 6: 12 men are drowned when the trawler *George Robb* runs aground at Duncansby Head in Scotland during a severe storm.

DECEMBER 1959

Monday 7: The American controlled city of Olangapo is ceded to the Philippines.

Tuesday 8: Nikita Khrushchev outlines proposals to build up the USSR's nuclear deterrent; the plans are made public in January 1960.

Wednesday 9: US President Dwight D. Eisenhower meets King Zahir Shah of Afghanistan *(left)* in Kabul; no US President visits the country again until 2006.

Thursday 10: The People's Republic of China begins a campaign to repatriate the global Chinese diaspora; approximately 100,000 people eventually return.

Friday 11: The CIA begins plans to assassinate Fidel Castro, with the first of several attempts taking place in July 1960.

Saturday 12: The first elections take place in Nigeria in anticipation of independence from Britain, scheduled for October 1960.

Sunday 13: Archbishop Makarios III is elected the first President of Cyprus following the island's independence from British rule.

Fidel Castro

DECEMBER 1959

Monday 14: Test pilot Joe Jordan sets the record for the highest altitude reached by a human to that date: 103,395 feet (19.6 miles) in an F-104 Starfighter.

Tuesday 15: Major Joseph W. Rogers, USAF sets the world air speed record, reaching 1,525.96 mph in an F-106 Delta Dart jet fighter.

Wednesday 16: The Supreme Court of Japan overturns a previous ruling that the presence of US forces in Japan is unconstitutional.

Thursday 17: Stanley Kramer's post-apocalyptic film *On the Beach*, starring Gregory Peck and Ava Gardner, premieres in 18 cities around the world.

Friday 18: The first communications satellite, Project SCORE, is launched from Cape Canaveral, playing a recorded message of goodwill from President Eisenhower.

Saturday 19: Mr Walter Williams of Houston, Texas, who claimed to be the last veteran of the American Civil War (1861-1865), dies aged supposedly 117. After his death his claim is disputed due to discrepancies in official records.

Sunday 20: BBC TV ends its long running series *Sunday Night Theatre*, which featured 721 plays over nine years.

DECEMBER 1959

Monday 21: The Royal Wedding takes place in Iran between Shah Mohammed Reza Pahlavi, 50, and 21 year old student Farah Diba.

Tuesday 22: Rock and roll singer Chuck Berry is arrested in St Louis, Missouri, over allegations of sex with a minor.

The Shah of Iran with Queen Farah

Wednesday 23: Stanford University heart surgeons Dr Richard Lower and Dr Norman Shumway perform a successful heart transplant between two dogs.

Thursday 24: Newly appointed Roman Catholic bishop, Karol Wojtyla (later Pope John Paul II) defies communist authorities by celebrating mass outdoors in Nowa Huta, the first Polish city to be constructed without a church.

Friday 25: In Seoul, South Korea, the commander of UN forces General Carter B. Magruder warns that North Korean forces may have developed nuclear weapons.

Saturday 26: The American explorers Edward C. Thiel, J. C. Craddock and E. S. Robinson become the first team to reach the Heritage Range of mountains in Antarctica, after they were discovered from the air on 14 December.

Sunday 27: Shah Mahmud Khan, former Prime Minister of Afghanistan, dies aged 69.

DECEMBER 1959

Monday 28: Children's animated television series *Ivor the Engine* is broadcast for the first time in the UK.

Ivor the Engine

Tuesday 29: US President Dwight D. Eisenhower announces that the USA will not renew the voluntary moratorium on nuclear testing between the USA, USSR and other nuclear powers, set to expire on 31 December.

Wednesday 30: The US Navy's first ballistic missile submarine, the USS *George Washington,* launched in June, goes into active service.

Eisenhower

Left: USS *George Washington*

Thursday 31: Actor Val Kilmer (*Batman)* is born in Los Angeles.

BIRTHDAY NOTEBOOKS

FROM
MONTPELIER PUBLISHING

Handy 60-page ruled notebooks with a significant event of the year on each page.

A great alternative to a birthday card.
Available from Amazon.

Printed in Great Britain
by Amazon